The
GREAT EASTERN
RAILWAY

Part One

A Selection of 7mm Locomotive Drawings

Compiled by M. Sharman

The
OAKWOOD PRESS

ISBN 0 85361 331 1

Published by
The OAKWOOD PRESS
P.O. Box 122,
Headington,
Oxford

INTRODUCTION

This is the third volume in the Portfolio series, compiled to give the railway historian and enthusiast the opportunity to collect (in a worthwhile scale of 7mm to the foot), most of the varied and interesting drawings contained within the pages of *The Locomotive Magazine*. This has been made possible by the kind co-operation of the magazine's owners, Ian Allan Ltd, Coombelands, Surrey.

These drawings are complementary to the many books that have been published over the years on the Great Eastern Railway and therefore can be studied in conjunction with them.

Accompanying each drawing is found the date and page number as to when it appeared in *The Locomotive Magazine* and this will aid your research further, if you should wish to read the article.

The range of drawings depicted in this volume is not in any way complete, in the sense that not all the GER classes are represented and a further two GER volumes are envisaged to give the reader a wider and more comprehensive selection.

These volumes on the GER and further volumes in the series are listed on the back cover and are grouped by Railway Companies or regions etc, where possible. It is proposed to include foreign railways in the series as so many of these locomotives were designed and constructed by British manufacturers, such as Sharp Stewart, Stephensons, Neilsons, Vulcan, Dubbs, etc.

I hope you find this third volume as exciting as the previous volumes and I look forward to presenting to you more drawings in future volumes.

M. Sharman 1987

BIBLIOGRAPHY

The Locomotive Magazine
The Engineer
The Railway Magazine
The Railway Engineer
HMRS Journals
The British Steam Locomotives 1825–1925 – Ahrons
Real photograph Collection of Ian Allan containing many GER locomotive
    photographs
Locomotives of the Great Eastern Rly. 1862–1962 – Aldrich
Great Eastern Locomotives, Past and Present 1862–195 – Aldrich
RCTS Volumes on the LNER

CONTENTS

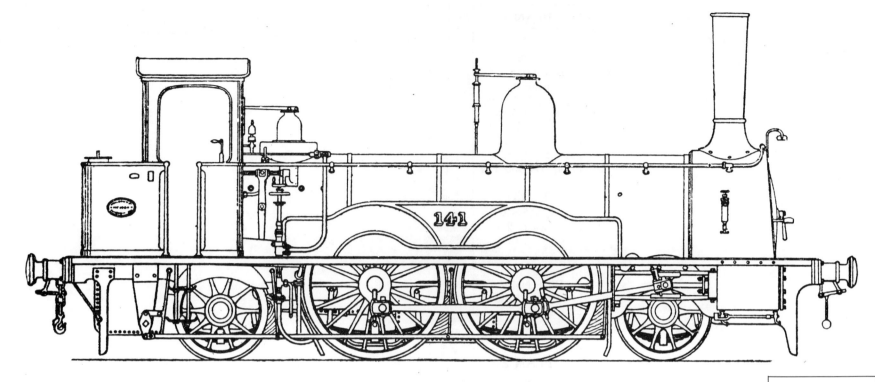

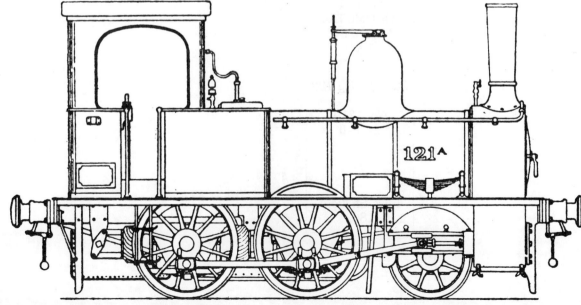

PLAN 1

This drawing
is reproduced
from the
LOCOMOTIVE
MAGAZINE
1909

Page 64, Fig. 131

**No.141
CLASS V
2–4–2**

Built: Neilson
& Co. 1864

PLAN 2

This drawing
is reproduced
from the
LOCOMOTIVE
MAGAZINE
1909

Page 44, Fig. 128

**No. 121A
2–4–0**

Built: Stratford
1862

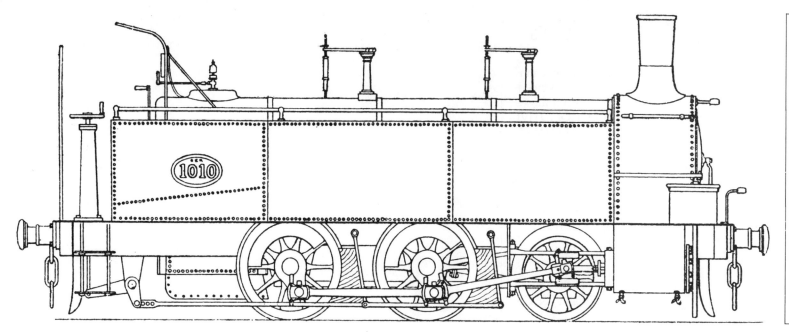

PLAN 3

★

This drawing
is reproduced
from the
LOCOMOTIVE
MAGAZINE
1909

Page 90, Fig. 136

**No. 1010
0–6–0T**

Built: Geo.
England & Co.
1860

PLAN 4

★

This drawing
is reproduced
from the
LOCOMOTIVE
MAGAZINE
1909

Page 107, Fig. 137

**No. 127
2–4–0**

Built: Neilson
& Co. 1867

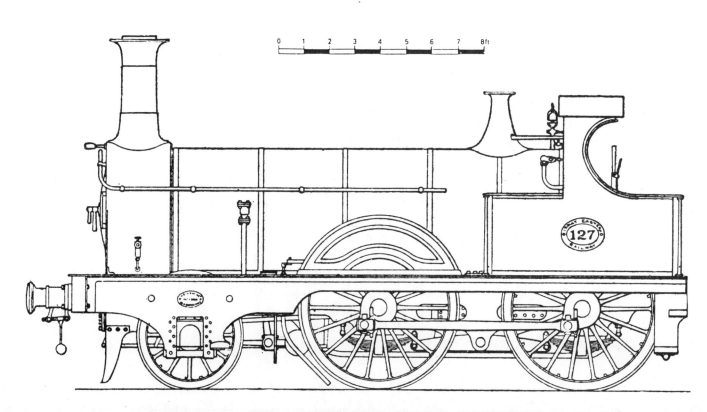

PLAN 3

★

This drawing
is reproduced
from the
LOCOMOTIVE
MAGAZINE
1909

Page 90, Fig. 136

No. 1010
0−6−0T

Built: Geo.
England & Co.
1860

PLAN 4

This drawing
is reproduced
from the
LOCOMOTIVE
MAGAZINE
1909

Page 107, Fig. 137

No. 127
2−4−0

Built: Neilson
& Co. 1867

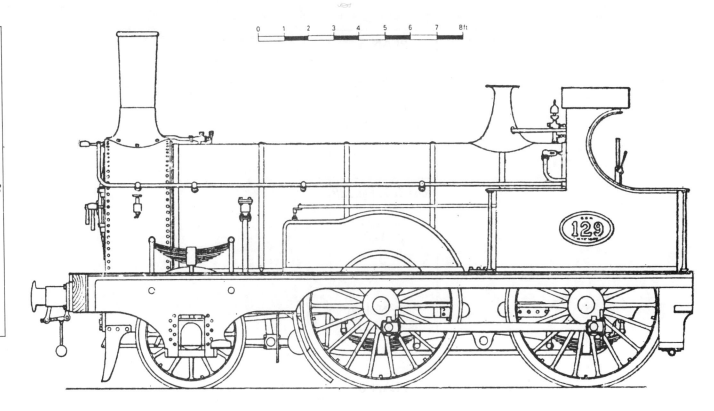

PLAN 5

★

This drawing
is reproduced
from the
LOCOMOTIVE
MAGAZINE
1909

Page 107, Fig. 138

**No. 129
2–4–0**

Built: Neilson
& Co. 1867

PLAN 6

★

This drawing
is reproduced
from the
LOCOMOTIVE
MAGAZINE
1909

Page 108, Fig. 139

**No. 201
0–6–0ST**

Built: Hudswell
Clarke & Co.
1867

PLAN 5

This drawing
is reproduced
from the
LOCOMOTIVE
MAGAZINE
1909

Page 107, Fig. 138

**No. 129
2–4–0**

Built: Neilson
& Co. 1867

PLAN 6

This drawing
is reproduced
from the
LOCOMOTIVE
MAGAZINE
1909

Page 108, Fig. 139

**No. 201
0–6–0ST**

Built: Hudswell
Clarke & Co.
1867

PLAN 7

★

This drawing
is reproduced
from the
LOCOMOTIVE
MAGAZINE
1909

Page 108, Fig. 140

**No. 202
0–6–0ST**

Built: Hudswell
Clarke & Co.
1867

0 1 2 3 4 5 6 7 8ft

PLAN 8

★

This drawing
is reproduced
from the
LOCOMOTIVE
MAGAZINE
1909

Page 131, Fig. 144

**No. 29
2–4–0**

Built: Sharp
Stewart & Co.
1868

PLAN 7

This drawing
is reproduced
from the
LOCOMOTIVE
MAGAZINE
1909

Page 108, Fig. 140

**No. 202
0−6−0ST**

Built: Hudswell
Clarke & Co.
1867

PLAN 8

This drawing
is reproduced
from the
LOCOMOTIVE
MAGAZINE
1909

Page 131, Fig. 144

**No. 29
2−4−0**

Built: Sharp
Stewart & Co.
1868

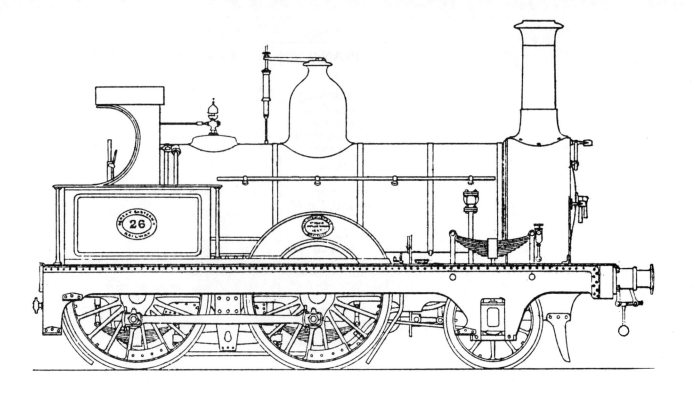

0 1 2 3 4 5 6 7 8ft

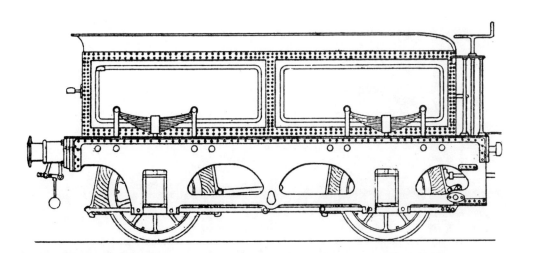

PLAN 9

★

This drawing
is reproduced
from the
LOCOMOTIVE
MAGAZINE
1909

Page 130, Fig. 141

No. 26
2 – 4 – 0

Built: Sharp
Stewart & Co.
1867

PLAN 9

This drawing
is reproduced
from the
LOCOMOTIVE
MAGAZINE
1909

Page 130, Fig. 141

No. 26
2-4-0

Built: Sharp
Stewart & Co.
1867

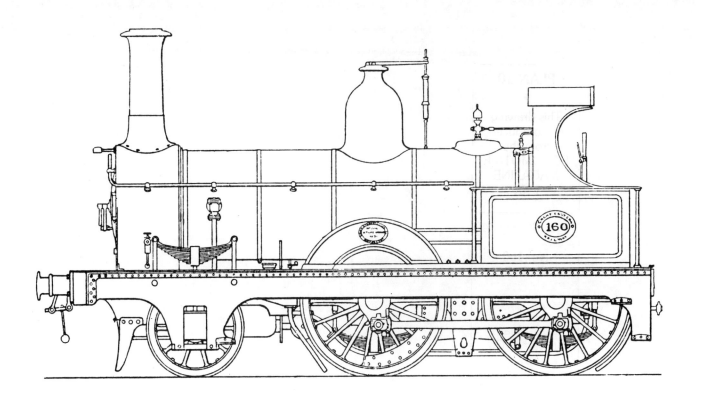

PLAN 10

★

This drawing
is reproduced
from the
LOCOMOTIVE
MAGAZINE
1909

Page 130, Fig. 142

No. 160
2 – 4 – 0

Built: Sharp
Stewart & Co.
1871

0 1 2 3 4 5 6 7 8ft

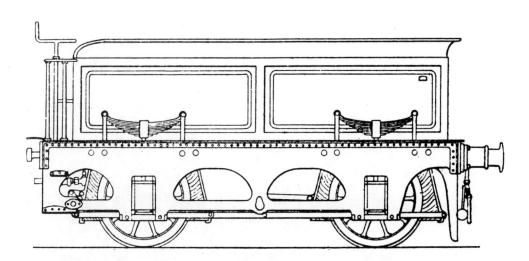

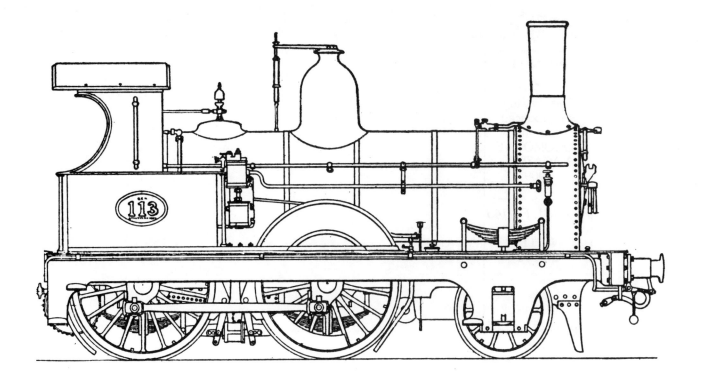

PLAN 11

★

This drawing
is reproduced
from the
LOCOMOTIVE
MAGAZINE
1909

Page 131, Fig. 143

No. 113
2−4−0

Built: Stratford
1869

0 1 2 3 4 5 6 7 8ft

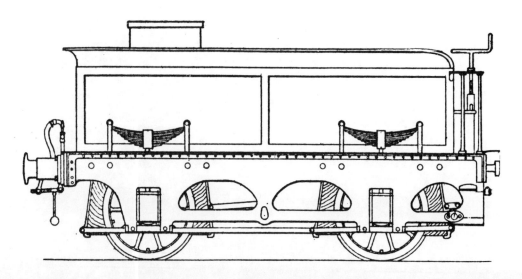

PLAN 11

★

This drawing
is reproduced
from the
LOCOMOTIVE
MAGAZINE
1909

_____

Page 131, Fig. 143

No. 113
2–4–0

Built: Stratford
1869

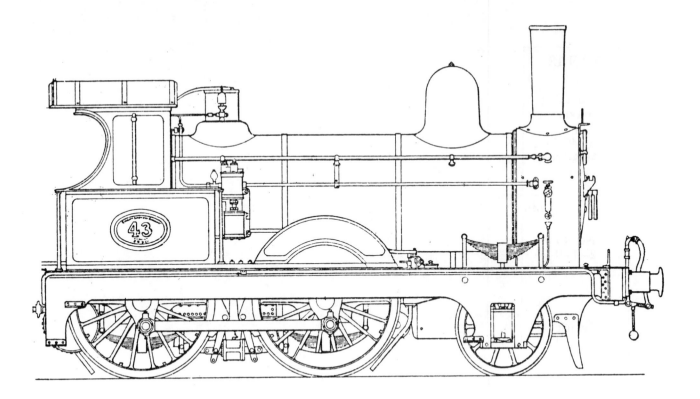

PLAN 12

★

This drawing
is reproduced
from the
LOCOMOTIVE
MAGAZINE
1909

Page 147, Fig. 145

**No. 43
2 – 4 – 0**

Rebuilt:
1889 – 93

0   1   2   3   4   5   6   7   8 ft

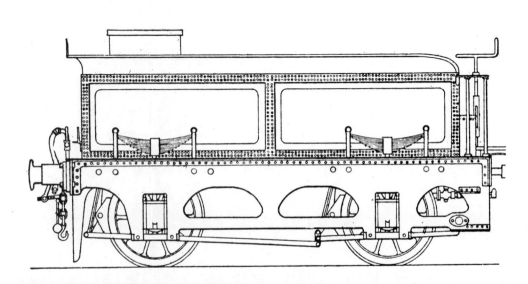

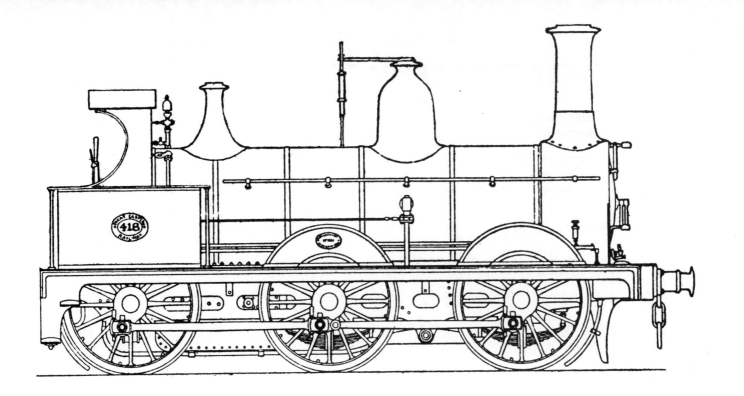

PLAN 13

★

This drawing
is reproduced
from the
LOCOMOTIVE
MAGAZINE
1909

Page 167, Fig. 146

**No. 418
0–6–0**

Built:
Neilson & Co.
1867

0   1   2   3   4   5   6   7   8ft

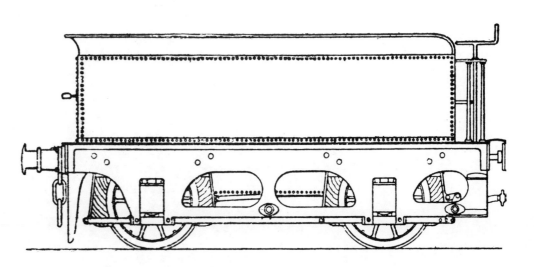

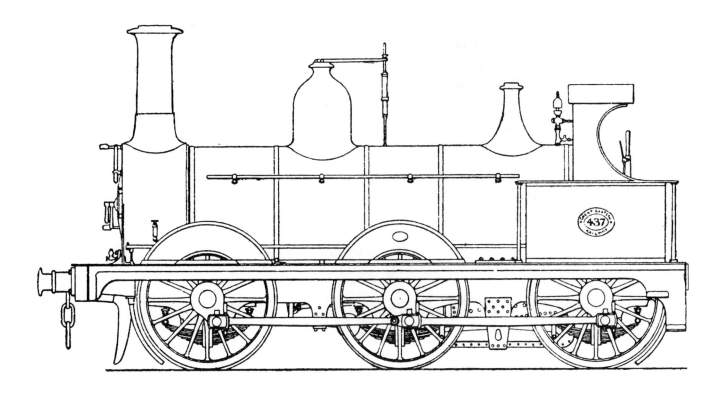

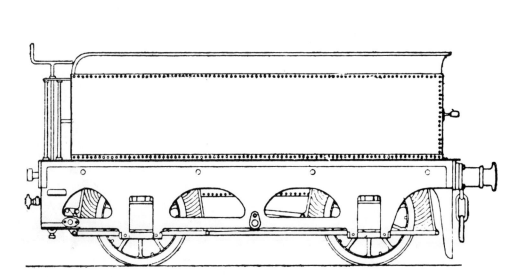

0 1 2 3 4 5 6 7 8ft

PLAN 14

★

This drawing
is reproduced
from the
LOCOMOTIVE
MAGAZINE
1909

Page 167, Fig. 147

N0. 437
0–6–0

Built: Worcester
Engine Co.
1867

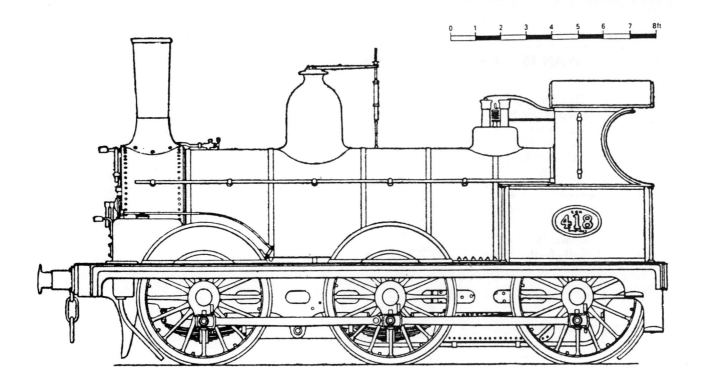

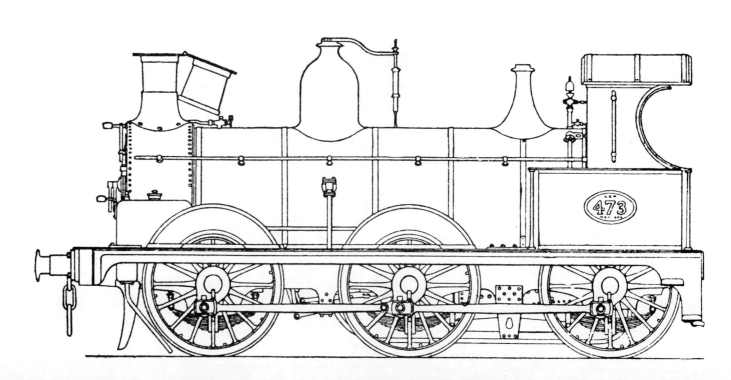

PLAN 15

This drawing
is reproduced
from the
LOCOMOTIVE
MAGAZINE
1909

———————

Page 168, Fig. 148

No. 418
0–6–0

Rebuilt:
1897

PLAN 16

This drawing
is reproduced
from the
LOCOMOTIVE
MAGAZINE
1909

———————

Page 185, Fig. 150

No. 473
0–6–0

Rebuilt:
1888

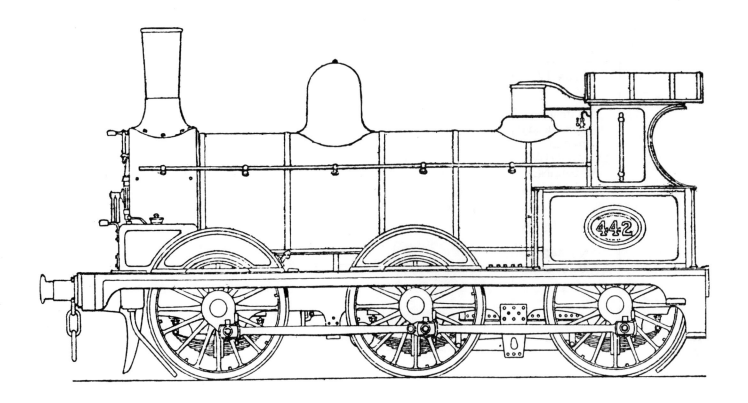

0 1 2 3 4 5 6 7 8ft

PLAN 17

★

This drawing
is reproduced
from the
LOCOMOTIVE
MAGAZINE
1909

Page 185, Fig. 149

No. 442
0–6–0

Rebuilt:
1885

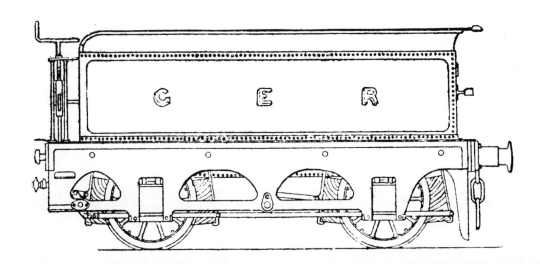

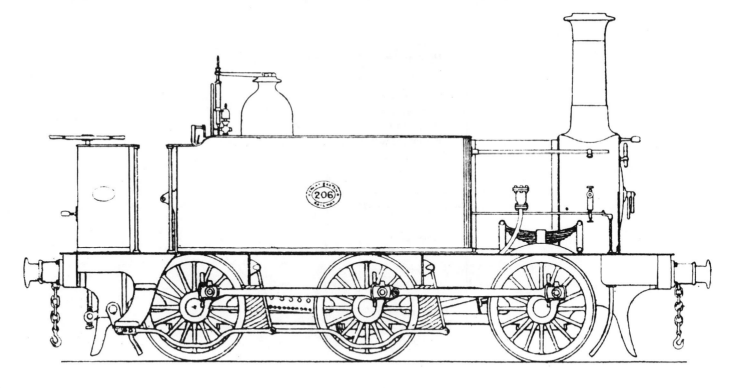

PLAN 18

★

This drawing
is reproduced
from the
LOCOMOTIVE
MAGAZINE
1909

Page 203, Fig. 151

**No. 206
0–6–0T**

Built: Ruston
Proctor & Co.
1868

206

0 1 2 3 4 5 6 7 8ft

PLAN 19

★

This drawing
is reproduced
from the
LOCOMOTIVE
MAGAZINE
1909

Page 203, Fig. 152

0–6–0ST

Rebuilt:
1881

PLAN 18

This drawing
is reproduced
from the
LOCOMOTIVE
MAGAZINE
1909

Page 203, Fig. 151

No. 206
0–6–0T

Built: Ruston
Proctor & Co.
1868

PLAN 19

This drawing
is reproduced
from the
LOCOMOTIVE
MAGAZINE
1909

Page 203, Fig. 152

0–6–0ST

Rebuilt:
1881

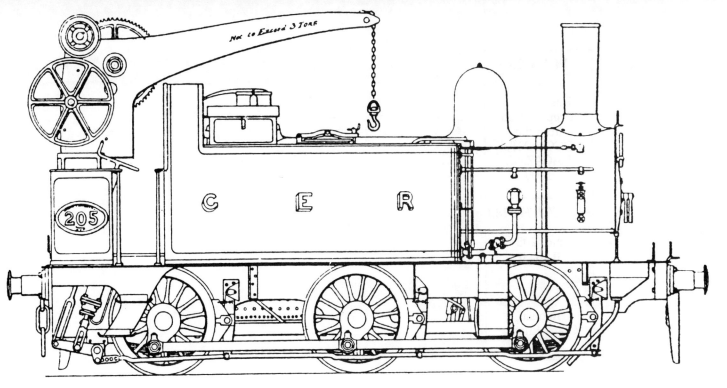

PLAN 20

★

This drawing
is reproduced
from the
LOCOMOTIVE
MAGAZINE
1909

Page 203, Fig. 153

**No. 205
0–6–0**

Rebuilt:
Crane Engine
1891

Not to Exceed 3 Tons

C   E   R

205

0 1 2 3 4 5 6 7 8ft

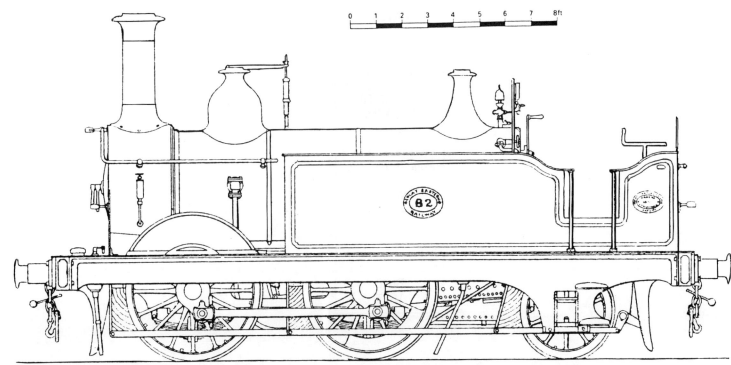

PLAN 21

★

This drawing
is reproduced
from the
LOCOMOTIVE
MAGAZINE
1910

Page 3, Fig. 156

**No. 82
0–4–2T**

Built:
1871

82

PLAN 20

★

This drawing
is reproduced
from the
LOCOMOTIVE
MAGAZINE
1909

Page 203, Fig. 153

No. 205
0–6–0

Rebuilt:
Crane Engine
1891

PLAN 21

★

This drawing
is reproduced
from the
LOCOMOTIVE
MAGAZINE
1910

Page 3, Fig. 156

No. 82
0–4–2T

Built:
1871

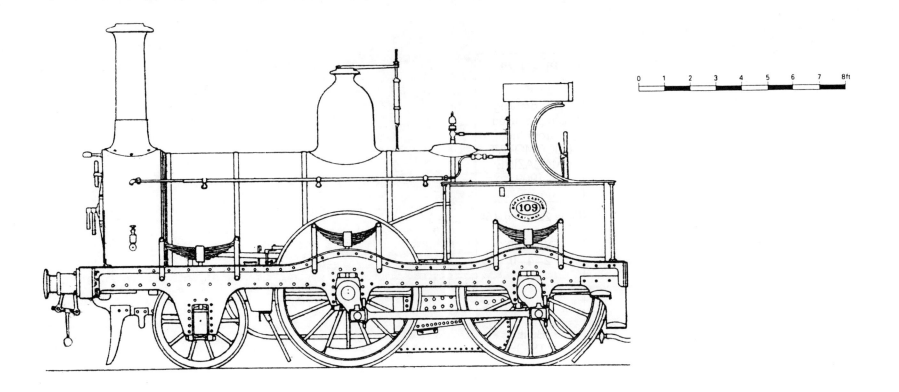

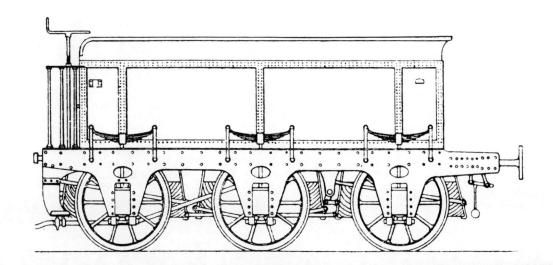

PLAN 22

★

This drawing
is reproduced
from the
LOCOMOTIVE
MAGAZINE
1909

Page 223, Fig. 154

No. 109
2–4–0

Built:
1863

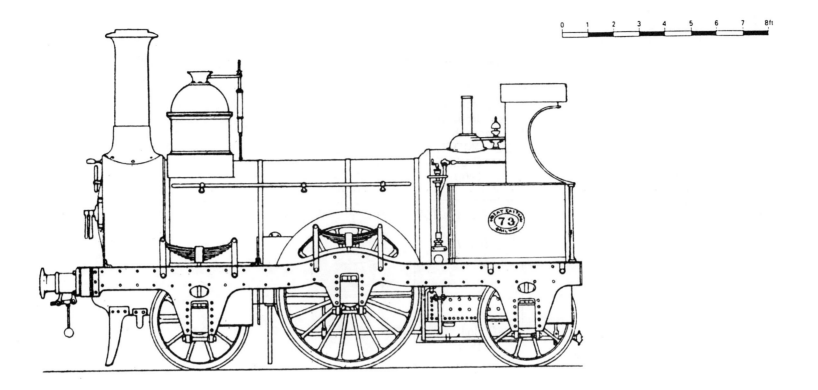

PLAN 23

★

This drawing
is reproduced
from the
LOCOMOTIVE
MAGAZINE
1909

Page 223, Fig. 155

**No. 73
2–2–2**

Built:
1870

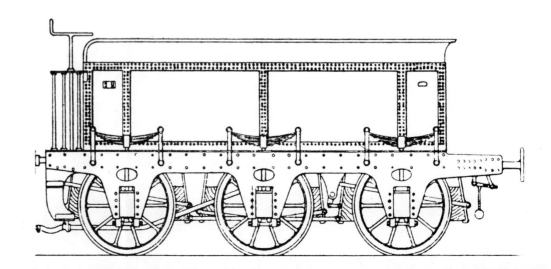

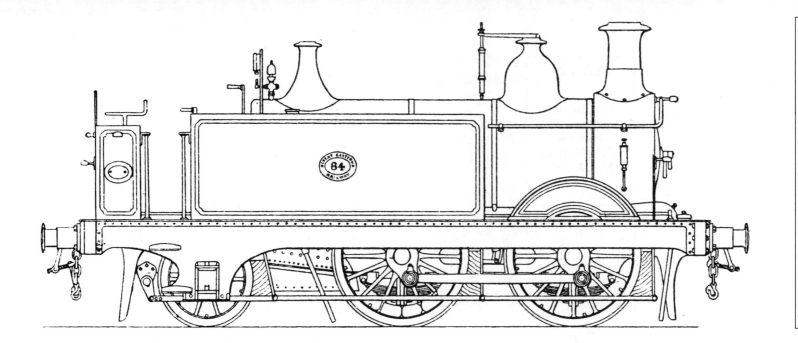

0 1 2 3 4 5 6 7 8ft

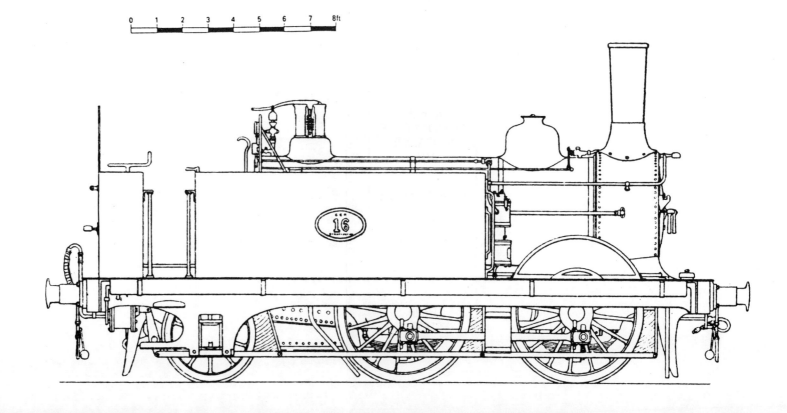

PLAN 24

This drawing
is reproduced
from the
LOCOMOTIVE
MAGAZINE
1910

Page 3, Fig. 157

**No. 84
0–4–2T**

Built:
1873

PLAN 25

This drawing
is reproduced
from the
LOCOMOTIVE
MAGAZINE
1910

Page 3, Fig. 158

**No. 16
0–4–2T**

Built:
1875

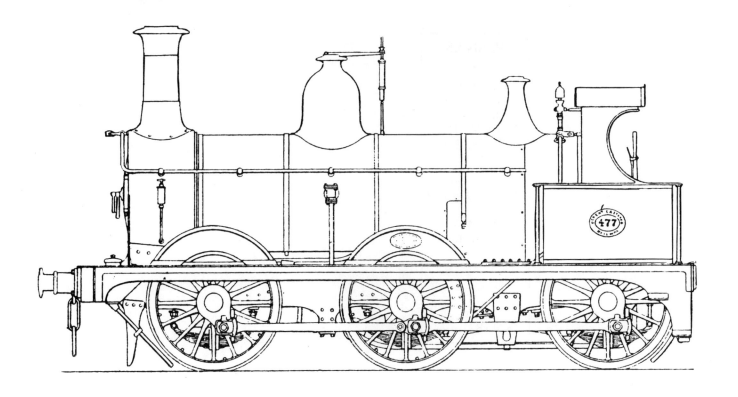

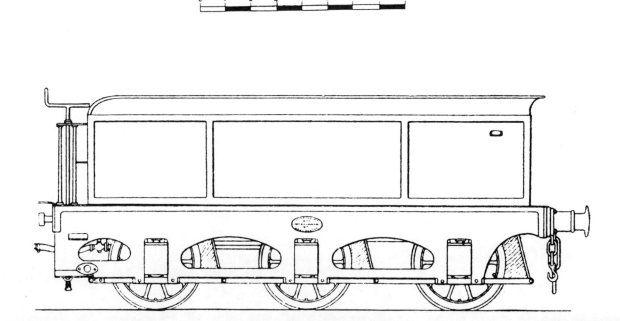

0 1 2 3 4 5 6 7 8ft

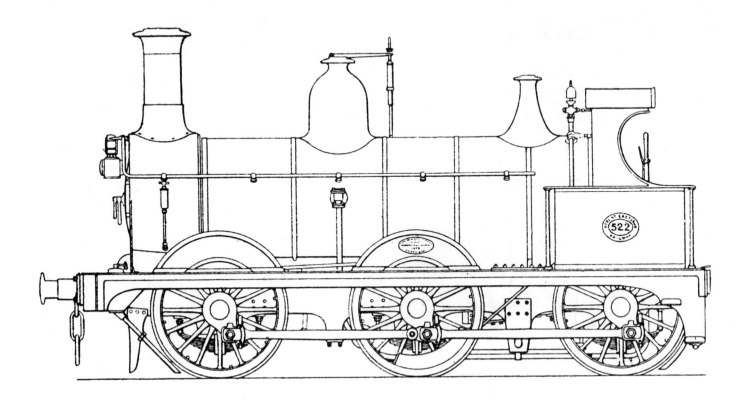

PLAN 27

★

This drawing
is reproduced
from the
LOCOMOTIVE
MAGAZINE
1910

Page 23, Fig. 160

**No. 522
0–6–0**

Built:
1873

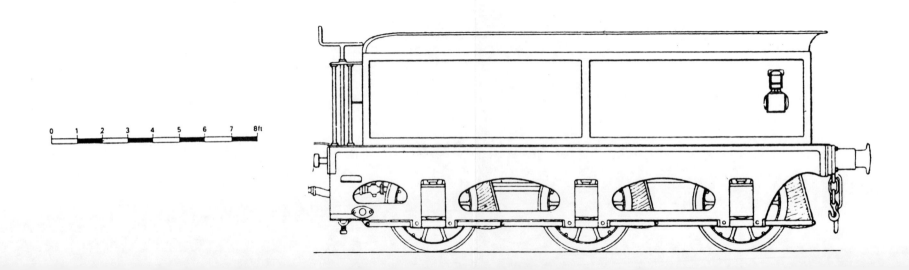

0 1 2 3 4 5 6 7 8ft

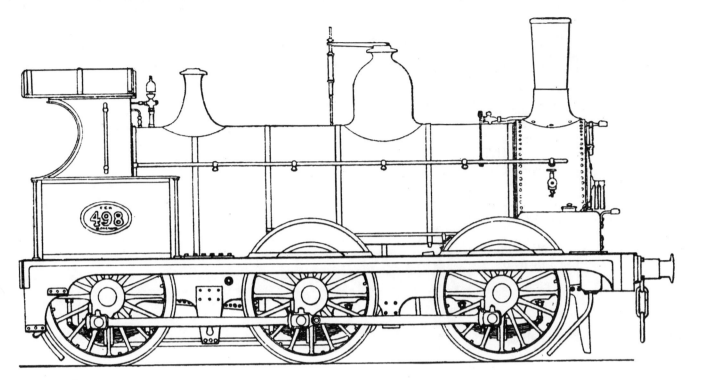

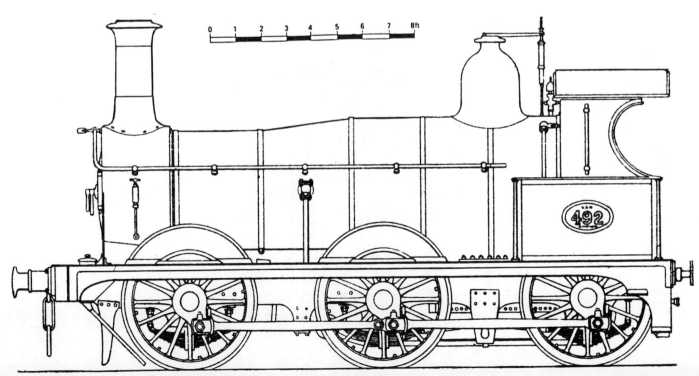

PLAN 28

★

This drawing
is reproduced
from the
LOCOMOTIVE
MAGAZINE
1910

Page 52, Fig. 161

**No. 498
0–6–0**

Rebuilt:
1879

PLAN 29

★

This drawing
is reproduced
from the
LOCOMOTIVE
MAGAZINE
1910

Page 52, Fig. 162

**No. 492
0–6–0**

Rebuilt:
1879

0 1 2 3 4 5 6 7 8ft

PLAN 28

This drawing
is reproduced
from the
LOCOMOTIVE
MAGAZINE
1910

Page 52, Fig. 161

No. 498
0–6–0

Rebuilt:
1879

PLAN 29

This drawing
is reproduced
from the
LOCOMOTIVE
MAGAZINE
1910

Page 52, Fig. 162

No. 492
0–6–0

Rebuilt:
1879

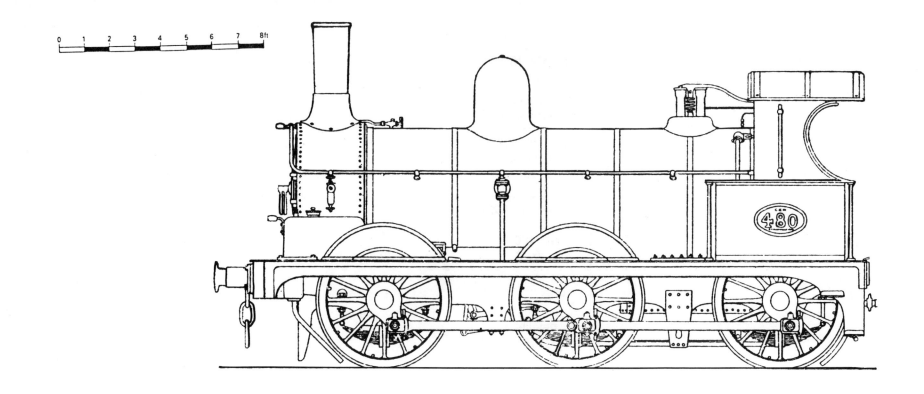

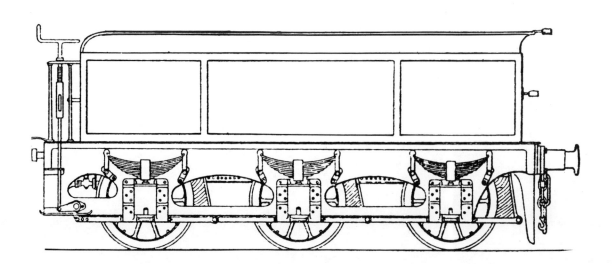

PLAN 30

★

This drawing
is reproduced
from the
LOCOMOTIVE
MAGAZINE
1910

Page 53, Fig. 164

**No. 480
0–6–0**

Rebuilt:
1879

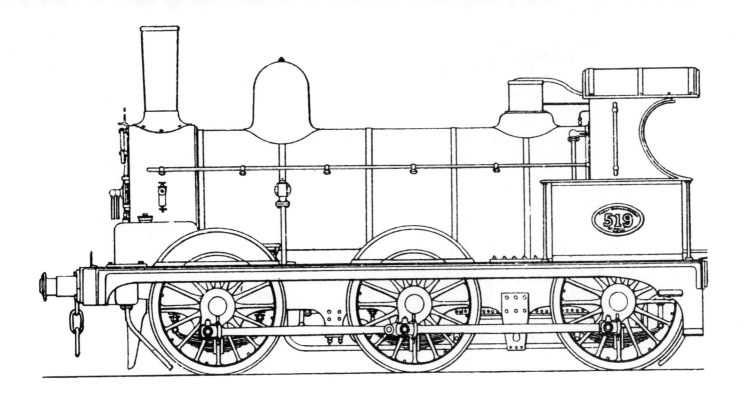

0 1 2 3 4 5 6 7 8ft

PLAN 31

★

This drawing
is reproduced
from the
LOCOMOTIVE
MAGAZINE
1910

Page 53, Fig. 165

**No. 519
0–6–0**

Rebuilt:
1892

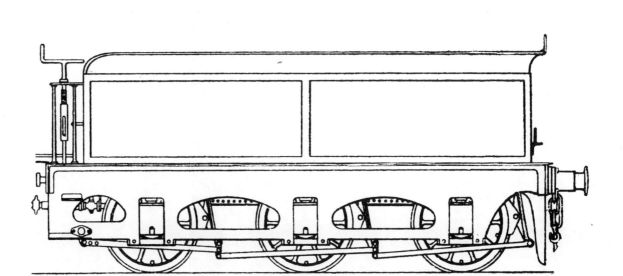

PLAN 31

★

This drawing
is reproduced
from the
LOCOMOTIVE
MAGAZINE
1910

Page 53, Fig. 165

No. 519
0–6–0

Rebuilt:
1892

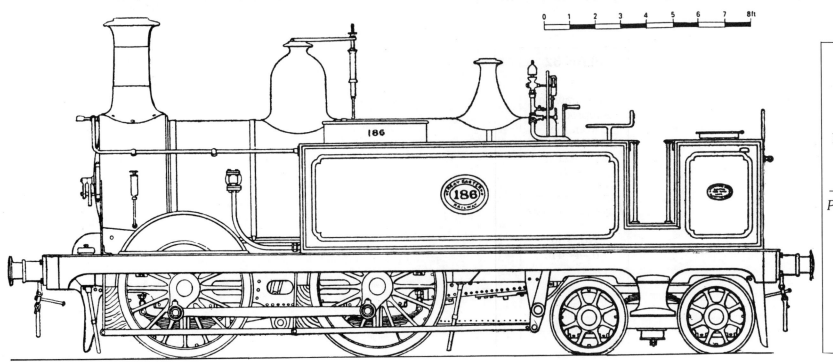

0 1 2 3 4 5 6 7 8ft

PLAN 32

★

This drawing
is reproduced
from the
LOCOMOTIVE
MAGAZINE
1910

Page 69, Fig. 167

**No. 186
0–4–4T**

Built:
Avonside
1872

PLAN 33

★

This drawing
is reproduced
from the
LOCOMOTIVE
MAGAZINE
1910

Page 70, Fig. 168

**No. 191
0–4–4T**

Built:
Avonside
1873

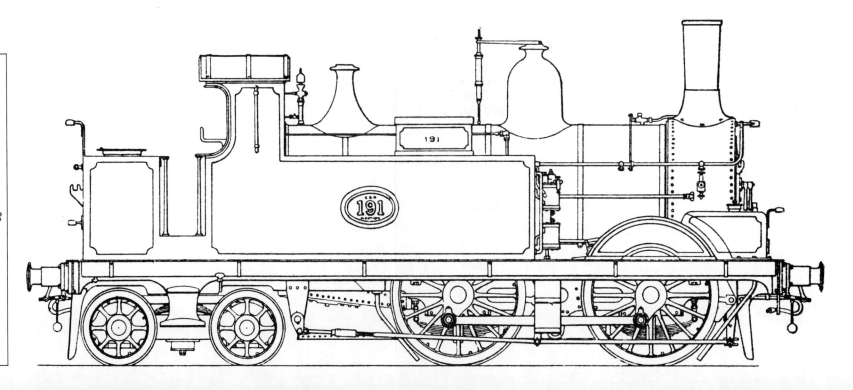

PLAN 32

★

This drawing
is reproduced
from the
LOCOMOTIVE
MAGAZINE
1910

Page 69, Fig. 167

**No. 186
0–4–4T**

Built:
Avonside
1872

PLAN 33

★

This drawing
is reproduced
from the
LOCOMOTIVE
MAGAZINE
1910

Page 70, Fig. 168

**No. 191
0–4–4T**

Built:
Avonside
1873

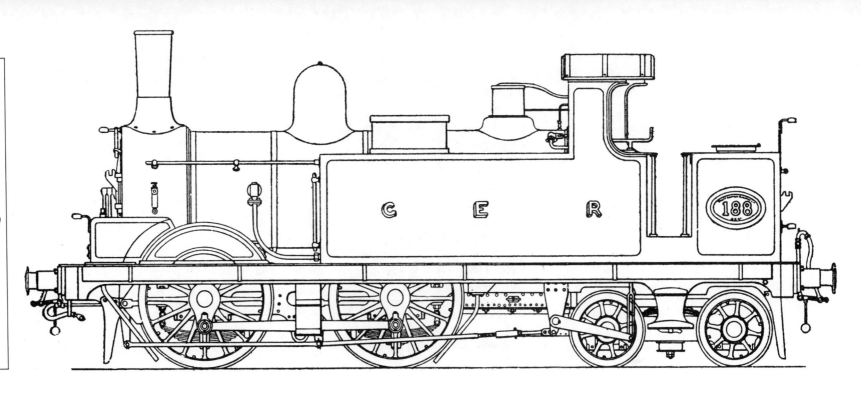

PLAN 34

★

This drawing
is reproduced
from the
LOCOMOTIVE
MAGAZINE
1910

Page 70, Fig. 169

No. 188
0–4–4T

Built:
Avonside
1872

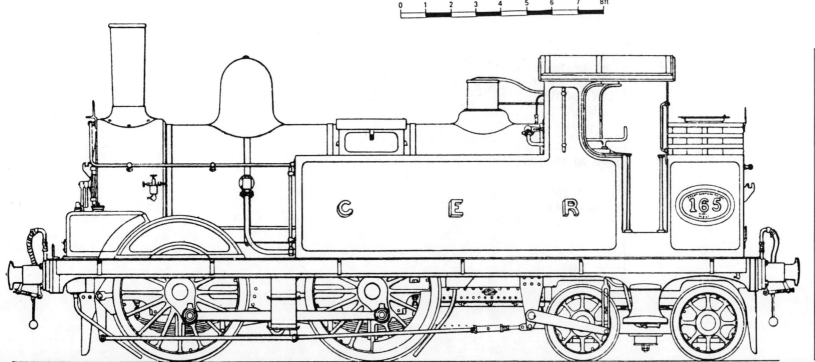

PLAN 35

★

This drawing
is reproduced
from the
LOCOMOTIVE
MAGAZINE
1910

Page 70, Fig. 170

No. 165
0–4–4T

Built:
Nielson & Co.
1872

PLAN 34

This drawing
is reproduced
from the
LOCOMOTIVE
MAGAZINE
1910

Page 70, Fig. 169

**No. 188
0−4−4T**

Built:
Avonside
1872

PLAN 35

This drawing
is reproduced
from the
LOCOMOTIVE
MAGAZINE
1910

Page 70, Fig. 170

**No. 165
0−4−4T**

Built:
Nielson & Co.
1872

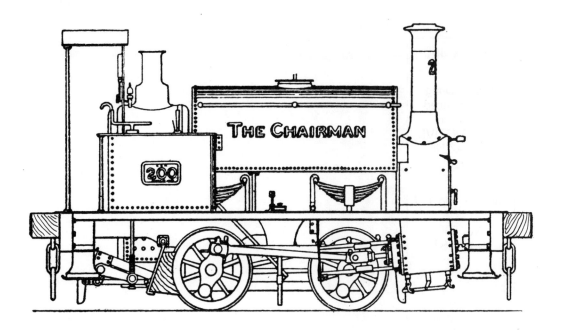

THE CHAIRMAN

200

PLAN 36

★

This drawing
is reproduced
from the
LOCOMOTIVE
MAGAZINE
1910

___

Page 92, Fig. 171

**No. 200
0–4–0ST**

Built:
Manning Wardle
1872

0 1 2 3 4 5 6 7 8ft

PLAN 37

★

This drawing
is reproduced
from the
LOCOMOTIVE
MAGAZINE
1910

___

Page 92, Fig. 172

**WORKS LOCO
0–4–0ST**

Rebuilt:
1895

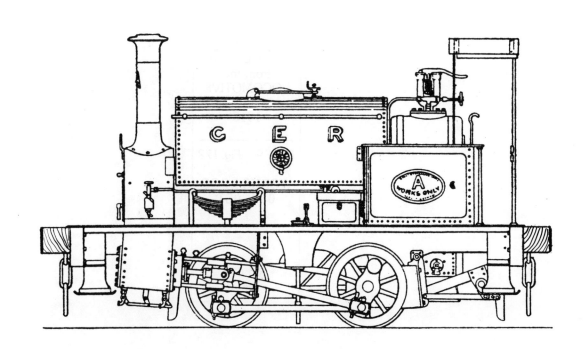

G E R

PLAN 36

★

This drawing
is reproduced
from the
LOCOMOTIVE
MAGAZINE
1910

Page 92, Fig. 171

No. 200
0−4−0ST

Built:
Manning Wardle
1872

PLAN 37

★

This drawing
is reproduced
from the
LOCOMOTIVE
MAGAZINE
1910

Page 92, Fig. 172

WORKS LOCO
0−4−0ST

Rebuilt:
1895

0 1 2 3 4 5 6 7 8ft

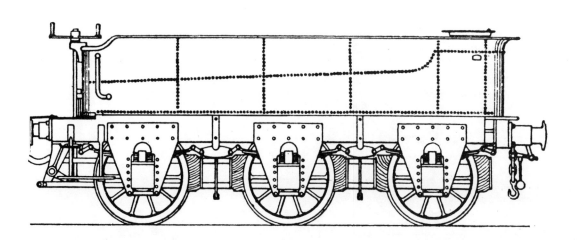

PLAN 38

★

This drawing
is reproduced
from the
LOCOMOTIVE
MAGAZINE
1910

Page 113, Fig. 173

No. 301
4–4–0

Built 1874 with
old Class 301
Tender

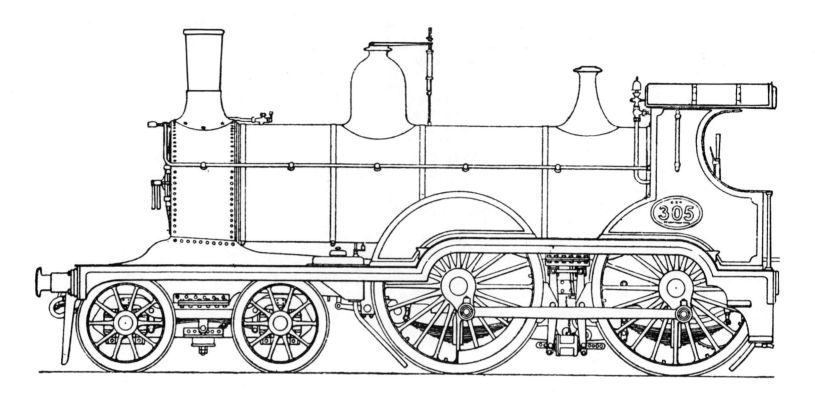

0 1 2 3 4 5 6 7 8ft

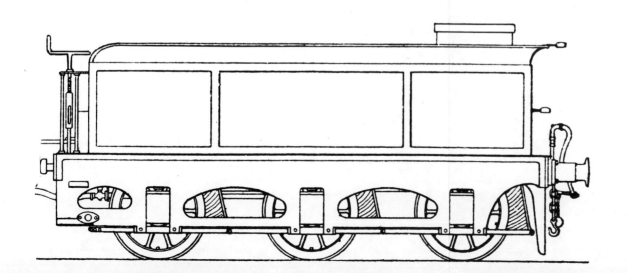

PLAN 39

★

This drawing
is reproduced
from the
LOCOMOTIVE
MAGAZINE
1910

Page 113, Fig. 174

No. 305
4–4–0

Rebuilt:
1878

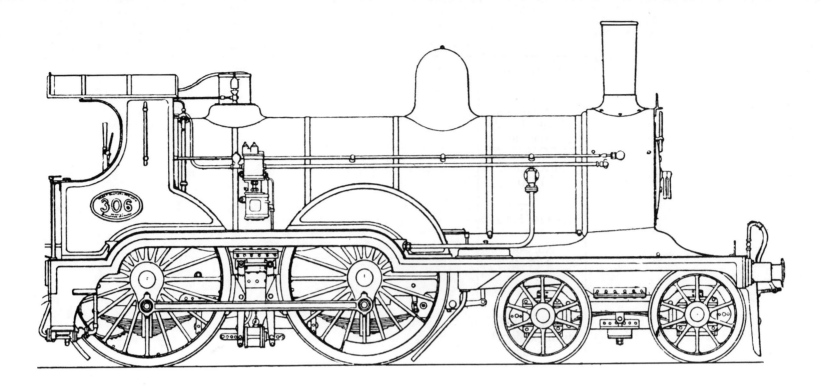

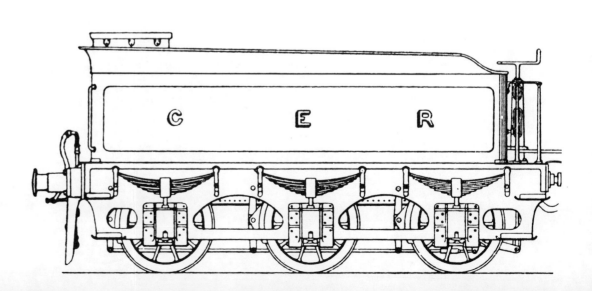

PLAN 40

★

This drawing
is reproduced
from the
LOCOMOTIVE
MAGAZINE
1910

Page 114, Fig. 175

No. 306
4–4–0

Rebuilt 1888
with ex Mogul
Tender

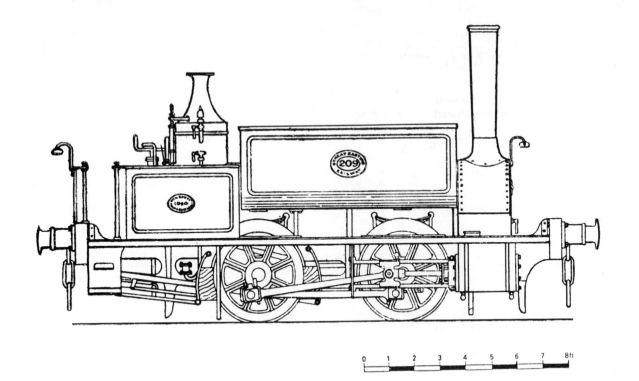

0 1 2 3 4 5 6 7 8ft

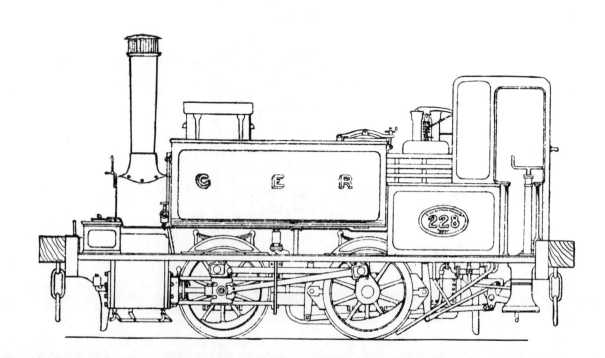

PLAN 41

This drawing
is reproduced
from the
LOCOMOTIVE
MAGAZINE
1910

Page 161, Fig. 176

**No. 209
0–4–0ST**

Built:
Neilson & Co.
1874

PLAN 42

This drawing
is reproduced
from the
LOCOMOTIVE
MAGAZINE
1910

Page 161, Fig. 177

**No. 228
0–4–0ST**

Rebuilt:
1894

PLAN 43

★

This drawing
is reproduced
from the
LOCOMOTIVE
MAGAZINE
1910

Page 185, Fig. 178

**No. 211
0–4–4T**

Built:
Neilson & Co.
1875

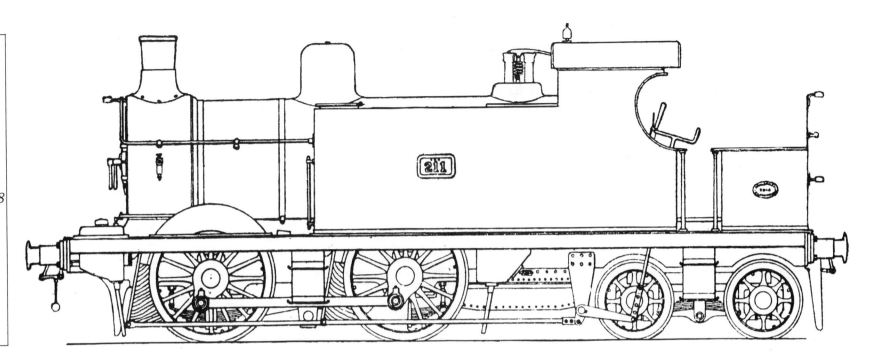

0 1 2 3 4 5 6 7 8ft

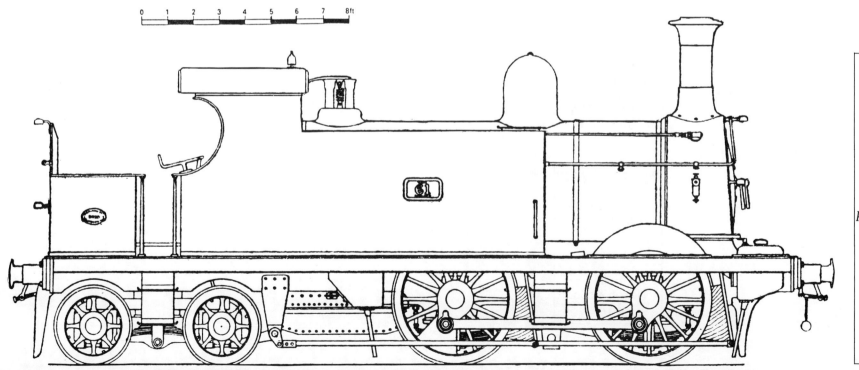

PLAN 44

★

This drawing
is reproduced
from the
LOCOMOTIVE
MAGAZINE
1910

Page 185, Fig. 179

**No. 61
0–4–4T**

Built:
Neison & Co.
1875

PLAN 43

★

This drawing
is reproduced
from the
LOCOMOTIVE
MAGAZINE
1910

Page 185, Fig. 178

**No. 211
0–4–4T**

Built:
Neilson & Co.
1875

PLAN 44

★

This drawing
is reproduced
from the
LOCOMOTIVE
MAGAZINE
1910

Page 185, Fig. 179

**No. 61
0–4–4T**

Built:
Neison & Co.
1875

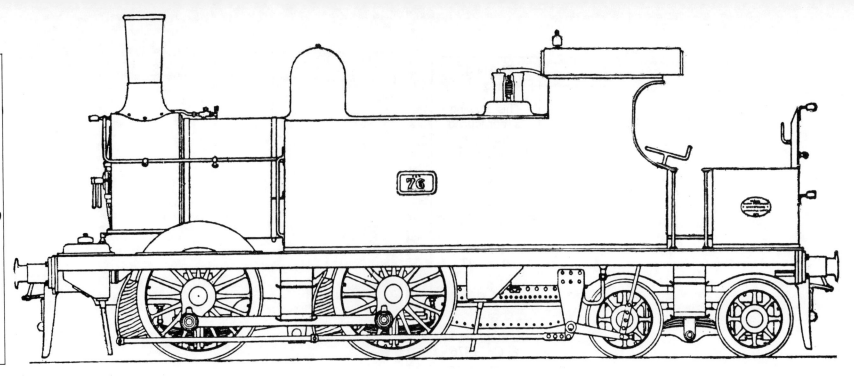

PLAN 45

★

This drawing
is reproduced
from the
LOCOMOTIVE
MAGAZINE
1910

Page 215, Fig. 180

**No. 76
0-4-4T**

Built:
R. Stephenson
& Co. 1876

0 1 2 3 4 5 6 7 8 ft

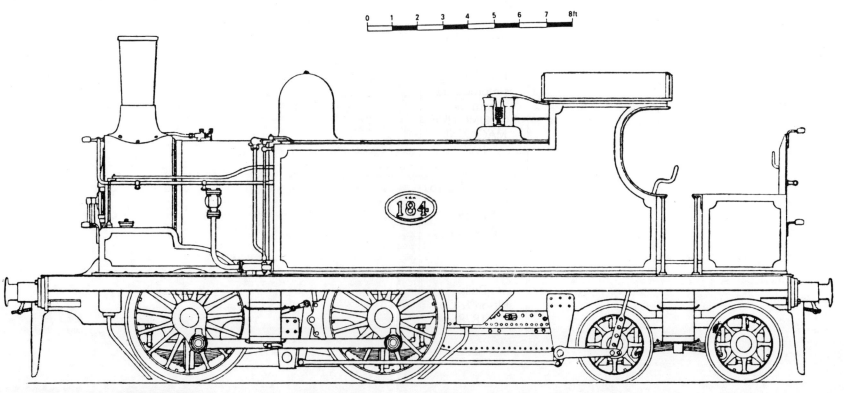

PLAN 46

★

This drawing
is reproduced
from the
LOCOMOTIVE
MAGAZINE
1910

Page 215, Fig. 181

**No. 184
0-4-4T**

Built:
Kitson & Co.
1878

PLAN 45

★

This drawing
is reproduced
from the
LOCOMOTIVE
MAGAZINE
1910

Page 215, Fig. 180

**No. 76
0–4–4T**

Built:
R. Stephenson
& Co. 1876

PLAN 46

★

This drawing
is reproduced
from the
LOCOMOTIVE
MAGAZINE
1910

Page 215, Fig. 181

**No. 184
0–4–4T**

Built:
Kitson & Co.
1878

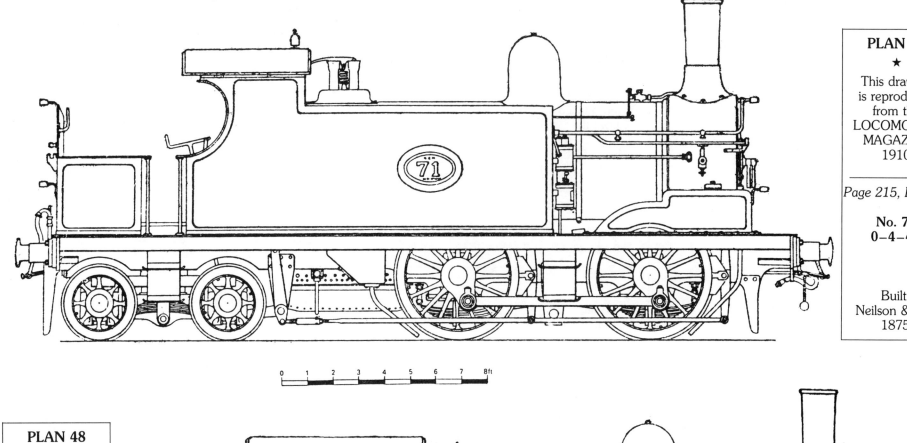

PLAN 47

★

This drawing
is reproduced
from the
LOCOMOTIVE
MAGAZINE
1910

Page 215, Fig. 182

No. 71
0–4–4T

Built:
Neilson & Co.
1875

0 1 2 3 4 5 6 7 8ft

PLAN 48

★

This drawing
is reproduced
from the
LOCOMOTIVE
MAGAZINE
1910

Page 216, Fig. 183

No. 66
0–4–4T

Rebuilt as
Oil Burner
1893

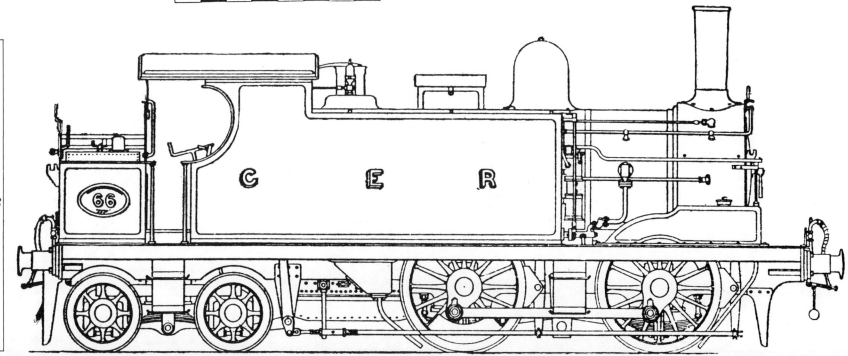

PLAN 47

★

This drawing
is reproduced
from the
LOCOMOTIVE
MAGAZINE
1910

_____

Page 215, Fig. 182

No. 71
0–4–4T

Built:
Neilson & Co.
1875

PLAN 48

★

This drawing
is reproduced
from the
LOCOMOTIVE
MAGAZINE
1910

_____

Page 216, Fig. 183

No. 66
0–4–4T

Rebuilt as
Oil Burner
1893

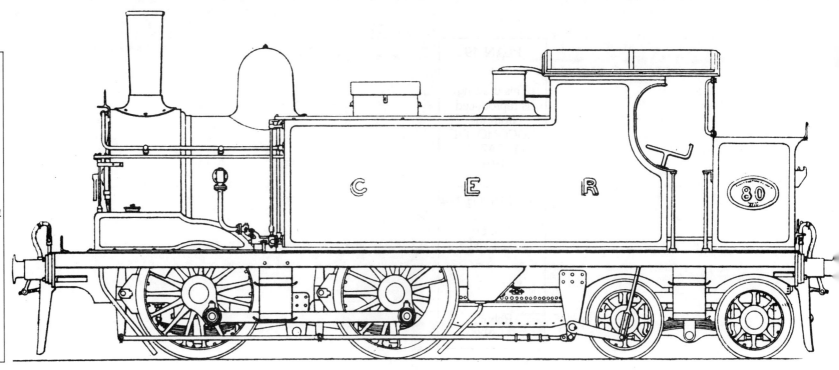

PLAN 49

★

This drawing
is reproduced
from the
LOCOMOTIVE
MAGAZINE
1910

Page 216, Fig. 184

**No. 80
0–4–4T**

Rebuilt:
1893

0 1 2 3 4 5 6 7 8ft

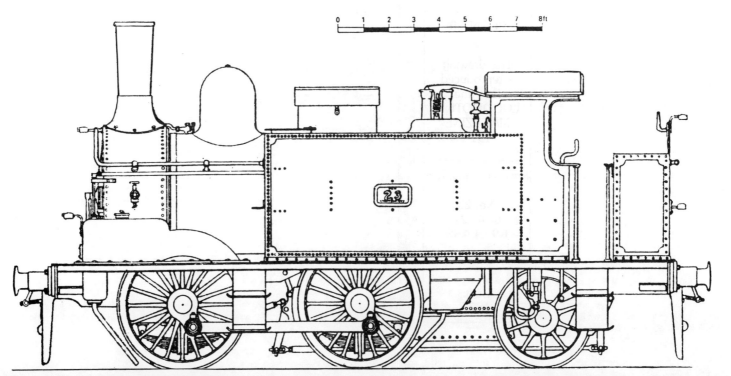

PLAN 50

★

This drawing
is reproduced
from the
LOCOMOTIVE
MAGAZINE
1910

Page 261, Fig. 188

**No. 23
0–4–2T
K9 CLASS**

Built:
1877

PLAN 49

This drawing
is reproduced
from the
LOCOMOTIVE
MAGAZINE
1910

Page 216, Fig. 184

**No. 80
0–4–4T**

Rebuilt:
1893

PLAN 50

This drawing
is reproduced
from the
LOCOMOTIVE
MAGAZINE
1910

Page 261, Fig. 188

**No. 23
0–4–2T
K9 CLASS**

Built:
1877

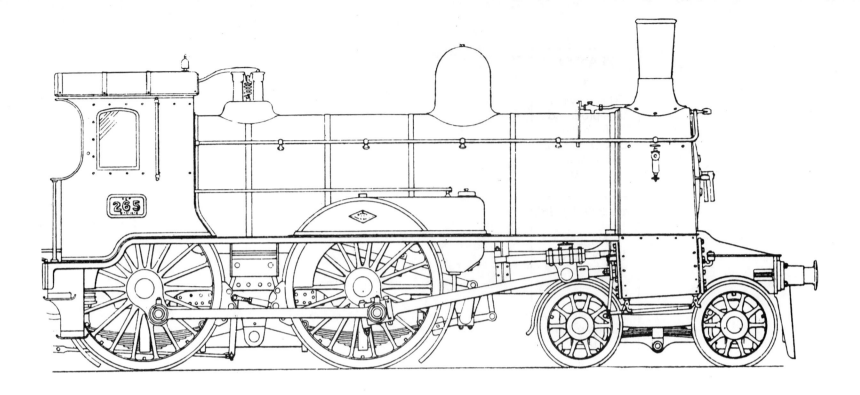

PLAN 51

★

This drawing
is reproduced
from the
LOCOMOTIVE
MAGAZINE
1910

Page 239, Fig. 185

No. 265
IRON CLADS

Built:
Dubs & Co.
1876

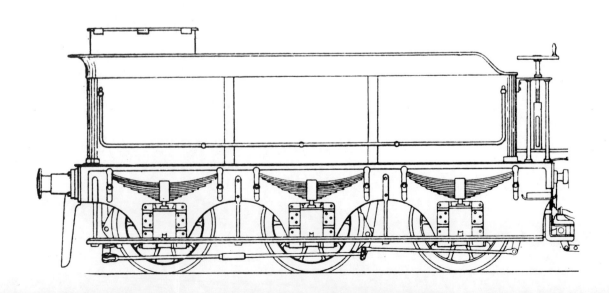

PLAN 51

This drawing
is reproduced
from the
LOCOMOTIVE
MAGAZINE
1910

Page 239, Fig. 185

No. 265
IRON CLADS

Built:
Dubs & Co.
1876

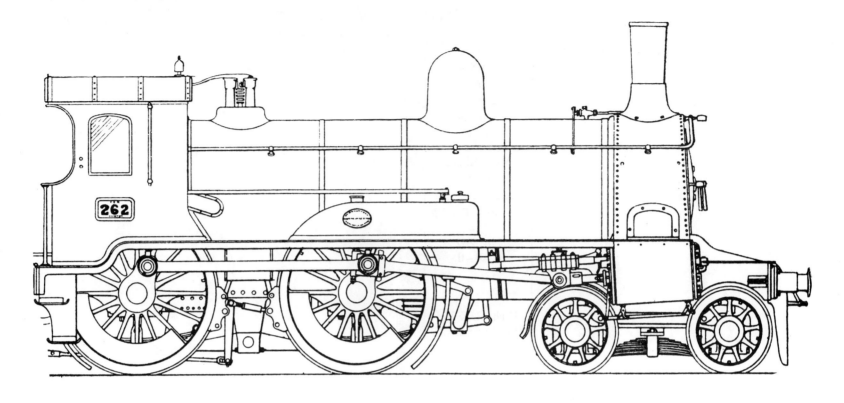

0 1 2 3 4 5 6 7 8ft

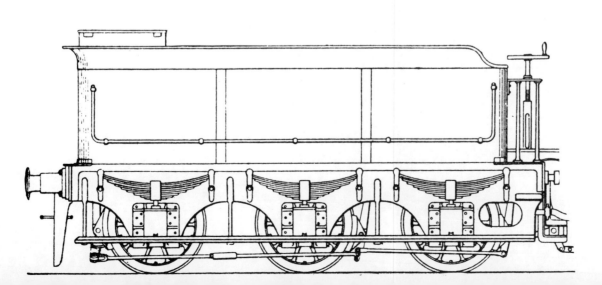

PLAN 52

★

This drawing
is reproduced
from the
**LOCOMOTIVE
MAGAZINE**
1910

Page 239, Fig. 186

**No. 262
4 – 4 – 0**

Built: R. & W.
Hawthorn & Co.
1877

PLAN 52

★

This drawing
is reproduced
from the
LOCOMOTIVE
MAGAZINE
1910

Page 239, Fig. 186

No. 262
4–4–0

Built: R. & W.
Hawthorn & Co.
1877

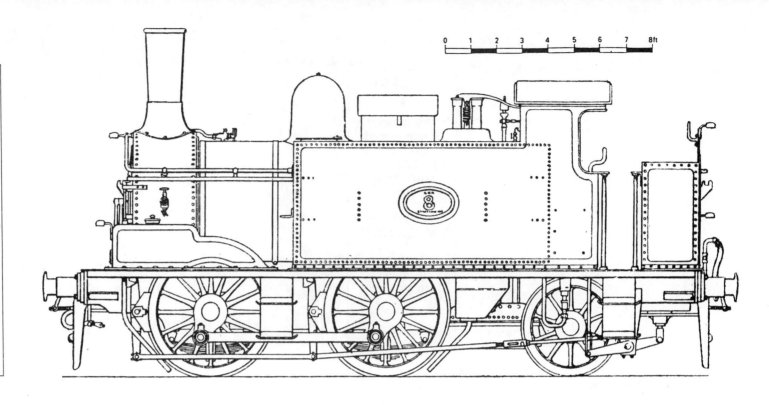

PLAN 53

★

This drawing
is reproduced
from the
LOCOMOTIVE
MAGAZINE
1910

Page 261, Fig. 189

**No. 8
0–4–2T
K9 CLASS**

Built:
1878

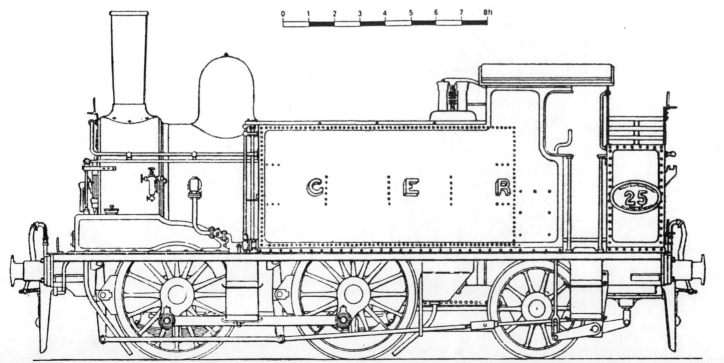

PLAN 54

★

This drawing
is reproduced
from the
LOCOMOTIVE
MAGAZINE
1910

Page 261, Fig. 190

**No. 25
0–4–2T
K9 CLASS**

Built:
1877

PLAN 53

This drawing
is reproduced
from the
LOCOMOTIVE
MAGAZINE
1910

Page 261, Fig. 189

**No. 8
0−4−2T
K9 CLASS**

Built:
1878

PLAN 54

This drawing
is reproduced
from the
LOCOMOTIVE
MAGAZINE
1910

Page 261, Fig. 190

**No. 25
0−4−2T
K9 CLASS**

Built:
1877

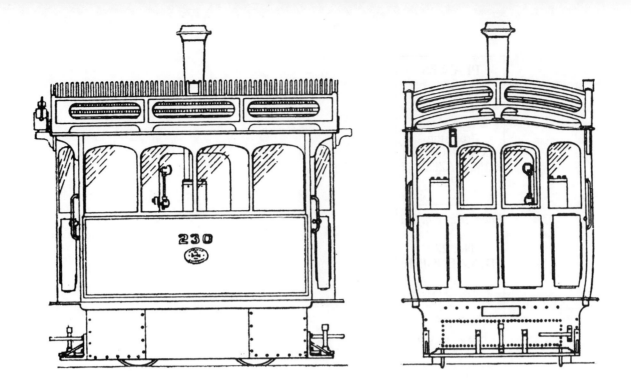

PLAN 55

★

This drawing
is reproduced
from the
LOCOMOTIVE
MAGAZINE
1910

Page 262, Fig. 191

**No. 230
TRAM ENGINE**

Built:
Kitson & Co.
1878

0   1   2   3   4   5   6   7   8ft

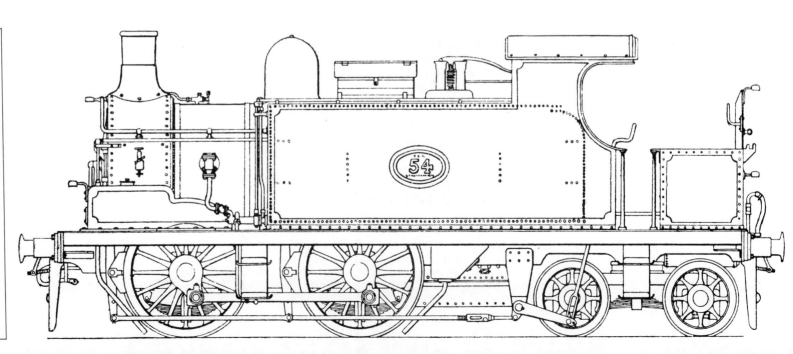

PLAN 56

★

This drawing
is reproduced
from the
LOCOMOTIVE
MAGAZINE
1911

Page 31, Fig. 193

**No. 54
0–4–4T
(E10 CLASS)**

Built:
1879

PLAN 55

This drawing
is reproduced
from the
LOCOMOTIVE
MAGAZINE
1910

Page 262, Fig. 191

**No. 230
TRAM ENGINE**

Built:
Kitson & Co.
1878

PLAN 56

This drawing
is reproduced
from the
LOCOMOTIVE
MAGAZINE
1911

Page 31, Fig. 193

**No. 54
0–4–4T
(E10 CLASS)**

Built:
1879

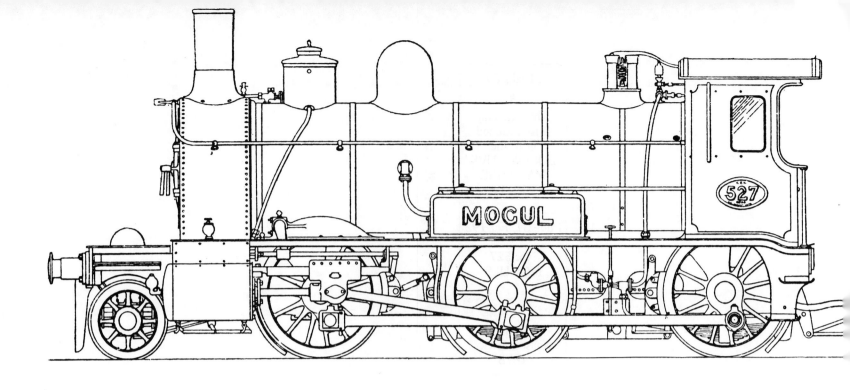

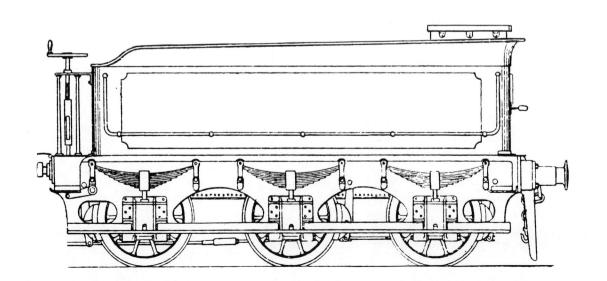

PLAN 57

★

This drawing
is reproduced
from the
LOCOMOTIVE
MAGAZINE
1911

Page 31, Fig. 192

**No. 527
MOGULS**

Built:
Neilson & Co.
1878

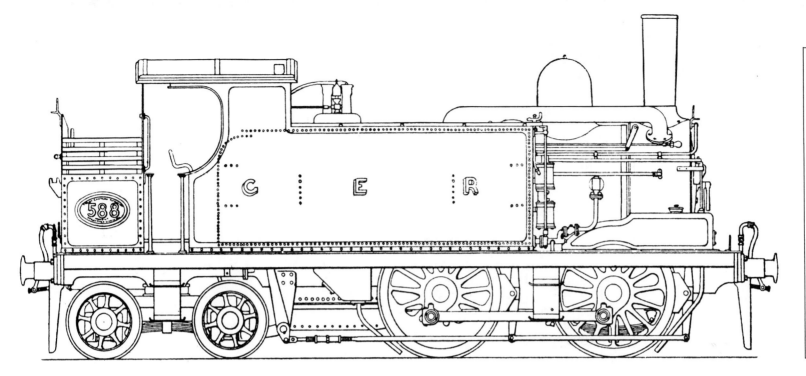

PLAN 58

★

This drawing
is reproduced
from the
LOCOMOTIVE
MAGAZINE
1911

Page 31, Fig. 194

**No. 585
0–4–4T**

Rebuilt:
1896

0 1 2 3 4 5 6 7 8ft

PLAN 59

★

This drawing
is reproduced
from the
LOCOMOTIVE
MAGAZINE
1911

Page 75, Fig. 198

**No. 203
0–6–0ST**

Built:
Hudswell Clarke
1876

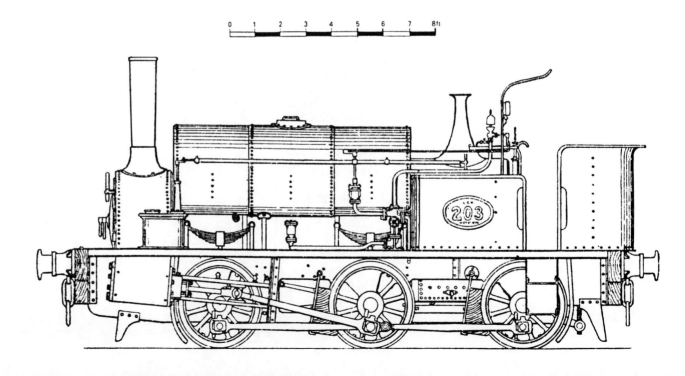

PLAN 58

This drawing
is reproduced
from the
LOCOMOTIVE
MAGAZINE
1911

Page 31, Fig. 194

**No. 585
0–4–4T**

Rebuilt:
1896

PLAN 59

This drawing
is reproduced
from the
LOCOMOTIVE
MAGAZINE
1911

Page 75, Fig. 198

**No. 203
0–6–0ST**

Built:
Hudswell Clarke
1876

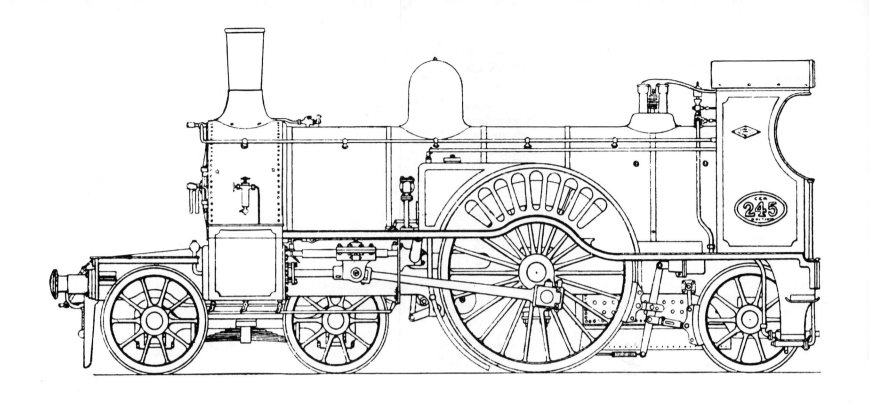

0 1 2 3 4 5 6 7 8ft

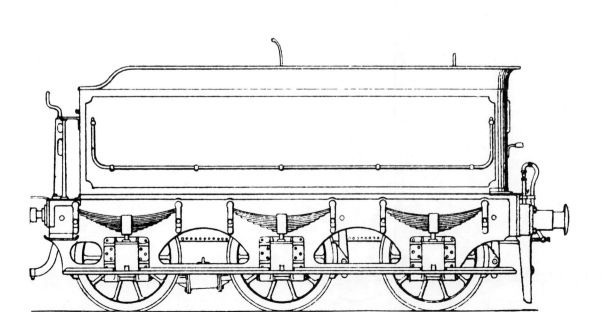

PLAN 60
★
This drawing
is reproduced
from the
LOCOMOTIVE
MAGAZINE
1911

Page 52, Fig. 195

No. 245
4–2–2

Built:
1879

PLAN 60

★

This drawing
is reproduced
from the
LOCOMOTIVE
MAGAZINE
1911

Page 52, Fig. 195

No. 245
4–2–2

Built:
1879

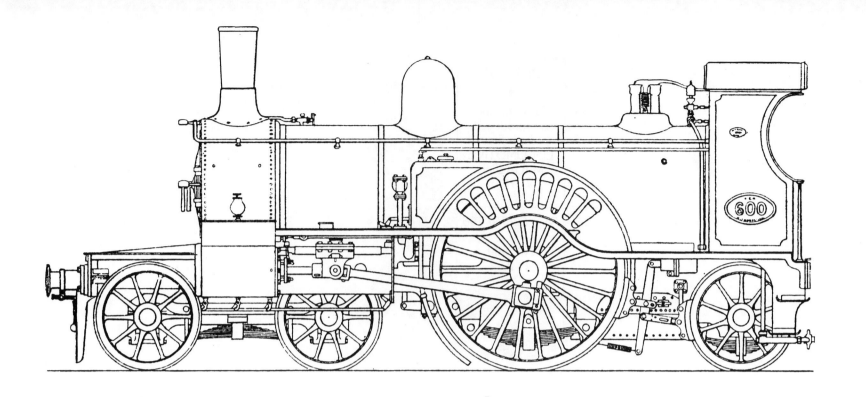

0 1 2 3 4 5 6 7 8ft

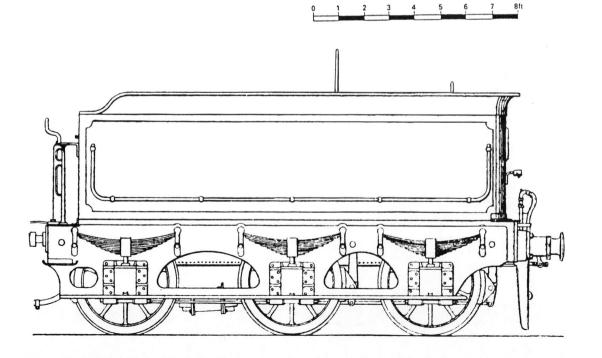

PLAN 61

★

This drawing
is reproduced
from the
LOCOMOTIVE
MAGAZINE
1911

Page 52, Fig. 196

**No. 600
4–2–2**

Built:
1881

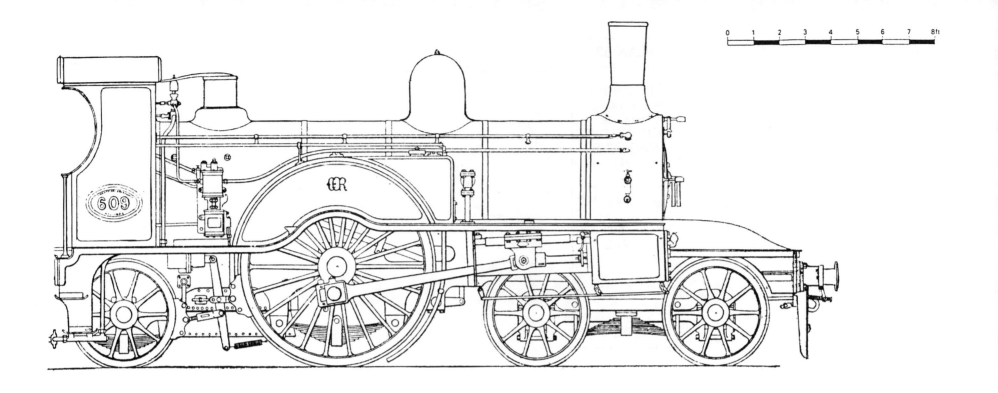

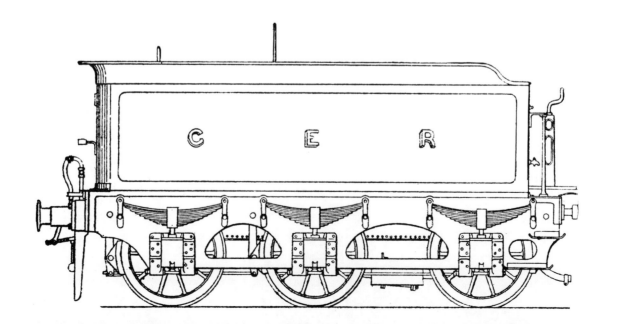

PLAN 62

★

This drawing
is reproduced
from the
LOCOMOTIVE
MAGAZINE
1911

Page 52, Fig. 197

**No. 609
4 – 2 – 2**

Built:
1882

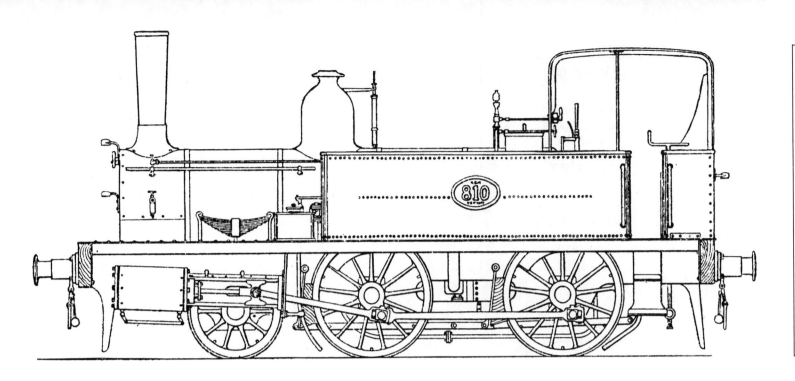

PLAN 63

★

This drawing
is reproduced
from the
LOCOMOTIVE
MAGAZINE
1911

Page 75, Fig. 199

**No. 810
2–4–0T**

Built: Yorkshire
Engine Co.
1887

0 1 2 3 4 5 6 7 8ft

PLAN 64

★

This drawing
is reproduced
from the
LOCOMOTIVE
MAGAZINE
1911

Page 76, Fig. 200

**No. 802
2–4–0T**

Built:
Manning Wardle
1870

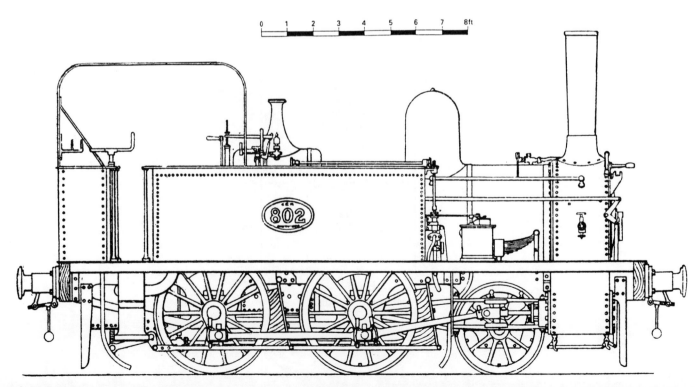

PLAN 63

★

This drawing
is reproduced
from the
LOCOMOTIVE
MAGAZINE
1911

———————

Page 75, Fig. 199

**No. 810
2–4–0T**

Built: Yorkshire
Engine Co.
1887

PLAN 64

★

This drawing
is reproduced
from the
LOCOMOTIVE
MAGAZINE
1911

———————

Page 76, Fig. 200

**No. 802
2–4–0T**

Built:
Manning Wardle
1870

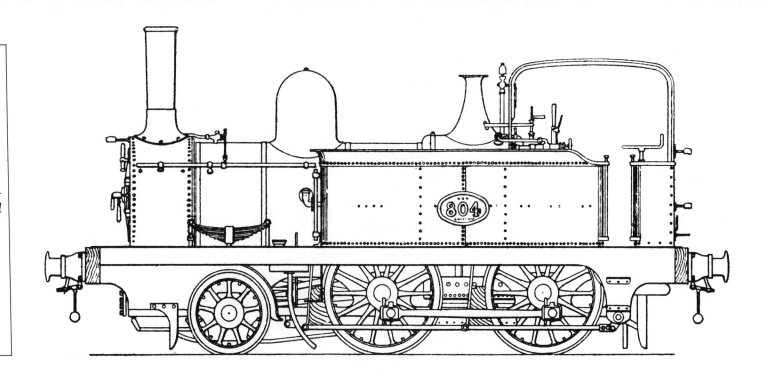

PLAN 65

★

This drawing
is reproduced
from the
LOCOMOTIVE
MAGAZINE
1911

Page 99, Fig. 201

**No. 804
2–4–0T**

Built:
Sharp Stewart
1875

0 1 2 3 4 5 6 7 8ft

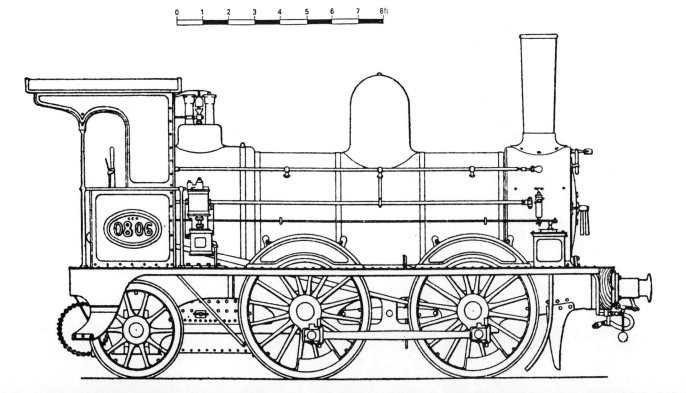

PLAN 66

★

This drawing
is reproduced
from the
LOCOMOTIVE
MAGAZINE
1911

Page 100, Fig. 203

**No. 806
0–4–2**

Rebuilt:
1886

PLAN 65

★

This drawing
is reproduced
from the
LOCOMOTIVE
MAGAZINE
1911

Page 99, Fig. 201

No. 804
2−4−0T

Built:
Sharp Stewart
1875

PLAN 66

★

This drawing
is reproduced
from the
LOCOMOTIVE
MAGAZINE
1911

Page 100, Fig. 203

No. 806
0−4−2

Rebuilt:
1886

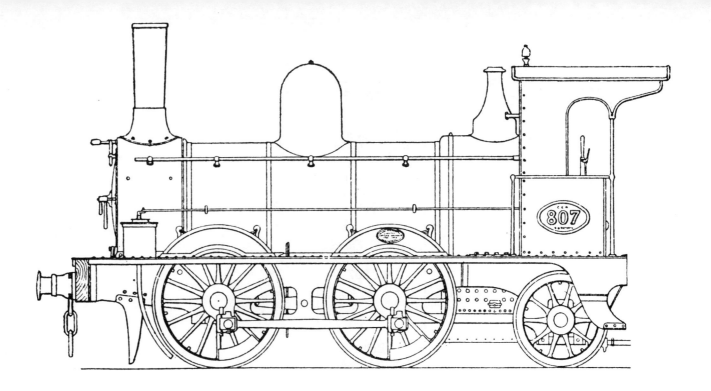

0 1 2 3 4 5 6 7 8ft

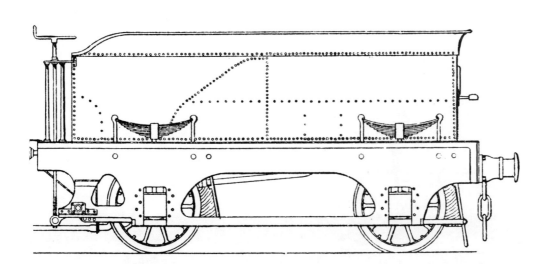

PLAN 67

★

This drawing
is reproduced
from the
LOCOMOTIVE
MAGAZINE
1911

Page 100, Fig. 202

**No. 807
0–4–2**

Built:
Sharp Stewart
1876

PLAN 67

★

This drawing
is reproduced
from the
LOCOMOTIVE
MAGAZINE
1911

Page 100, Fig. 202

No. 807
0–4–2

Built:
Sharp Stewart
1876

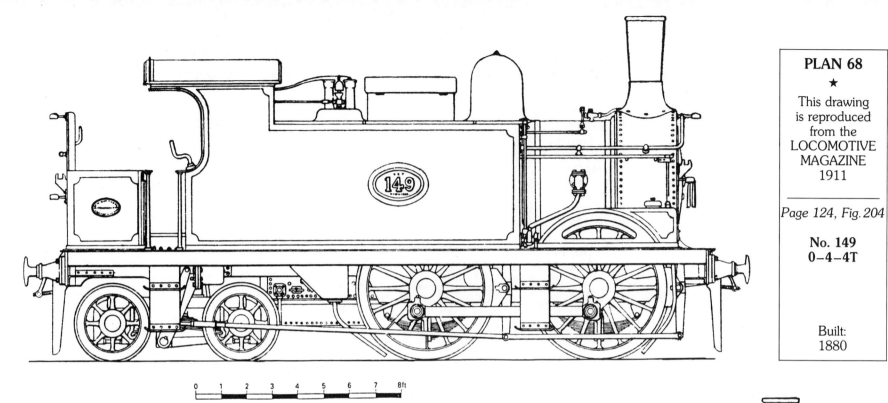

PLAN 68

★

This drawing
is reproduced
from the
LOCOMOTIVE
MAGAZINE
1911

Page 124, Fig. 204

**No. 149
0–4–4T**

Built:
1880

0 1 2 3 4 5 6 7 8ft

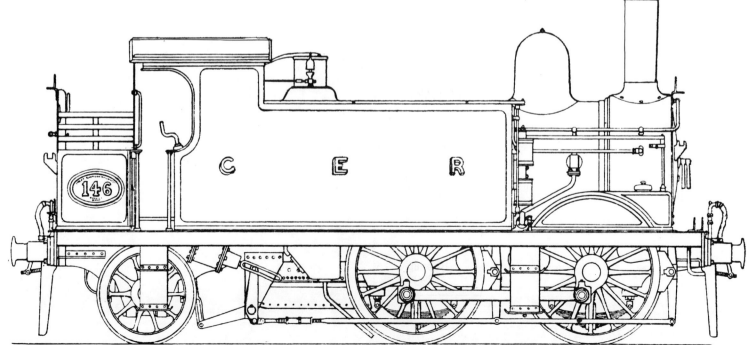

PLAN 69

★

This drawing
is reproduced
from the
LOCOMOTIVE
MAGAZINE
1911

Page 125, Fig. 205

**No. 146
0–4–2T**

Rebuilt:
1890

PLAN 68

★

This drawing
is reproduced
from the
LOCOMOTIVE
MAGAZINE
1911

Page 124, Fig. 204

**No. 149
0−4−4T**

Built:
1880

PLAN 69

★

This drawing
is reproduced
from the
LOCOMOTIVE
MAGAZINE
1911

Page 125, Fig. 205

**No. 146
0−4−2T**

Rebuilt:
1890

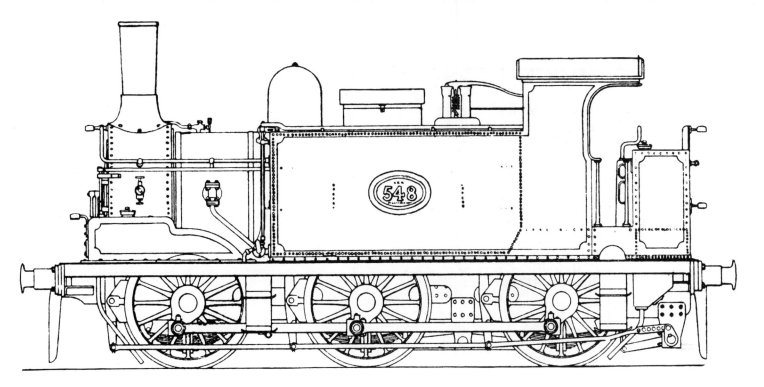

PLAN 70

★

This drawing
is reproduced
from the
LOCOMOTIVE
MAGAZINE
1911

Page 173, Fig. 206

**No. 548
0–6–0T
(CLASS M12)**

Built:
1881

0 1 2 3 4 5 6 7 8ft

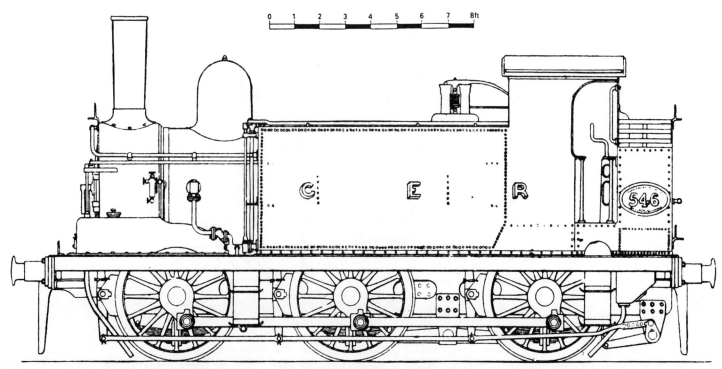

PLAN 71

★

This drawing
is reproduced
from the
LOCOMOTIVE
MAGAZINE
1911

Page 173, Fig. 207

**No. 546
0–6–0T
(CLASS M12)**

Rebuilt:
1895

PLAN 70

This drawing
is reproduced
from the
LOCOMOTIVE
MAGAZINE
1911

Page 173, Fig. 206

**No. 548
0–6–0T
(CLASS M12)**

Built:
1881

PLAN 71

This drawing
is reproduced
from the
LOCOMOTIVE
MAGAZINE
1911

Page 173, Fig. 207

**No. 546
0–6–0T
(CLASS M12)**

Rebuilt:
1895

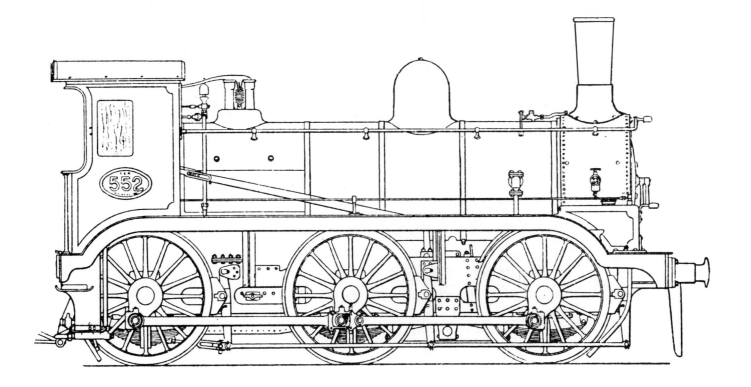

0 1 2 3 4 5 6 7 8ft

PLAN 72

★

This drawing
is reproduced
from the
LOCOMOTIVE
MAGAZINE
1911

Page 173, Fig. 208

No. 552
0–6–0

Built:
1882

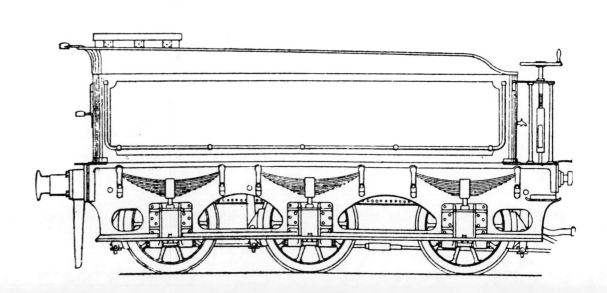

PLAN 72

★

This drawing
is reproduced
from the
LOCOMOTIVE
MAGAZINE
1911

Page 173, Fig. 208

No. 552
0−6−0

Built:
1882

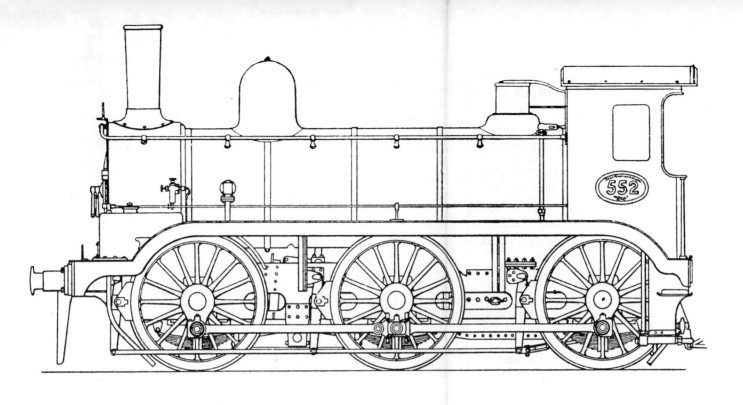

0 1 2 3 4 5 6 7 8ft

PLAN 73

★

This drawing
is reproduced
from the
LOCOMOTIVE
MAGAZINE
1911

Page 174, Fig. 209

No. 552
0–6–0

Rebuilt:
1893

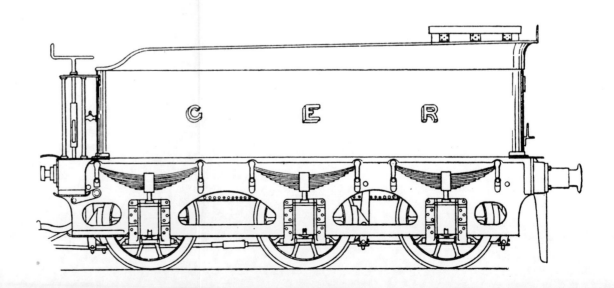